NFL's TOP 10
COMEBACKS

by Brian Hall

NFL's TOP TEN

SportsZone

An Imprint of Abdo Publishing
abdopublishing.com

abdopublishing.com

Published by Abdo Publishing, a division of ABDO, PO Box 398166, Minneapolis, Minnesota 55439. Copyright © 2018 by Abdo Consulting Group, Inc. International copyrights reserved in all countries. No part of this book may be reproduced in any form without written permission from the publisher. SportsZone™ is a trademark and logo of Abdo Publishing.

Printed in the United States of America, North Mankato, Minnesota
042017
092017

Cover Photo: Gregory Payan/AP Images
Interior Photos: G. Newman Lowrance/AP Images, 4–5; Ben Margot/AP Images, 6–7; Mark Zaleski/AP Images, 8, 9; Richard Mackson/Sports Illustrated/Getty Images, 11; John T. Greilick/AP Images, 13; Roy Dabner/AP Images, 14; Paul Connors/AP Images, 15; Ron Heflin/AP Images, 17; Tony Tomsic/Sports Illustrated/Getty Images, 18; Allen Kee/Getty Images Sport/Getty Images, 18–19; Scott Boehm/AP Images, 21; John Biever/Sports Illustrated/Getty Images, 22–23; Chuck Burton/AP Images, 24; Matt Slocum/AP Images, 25; Sean Ryan/IPS/Rex Features/AP Images, 26; Dave Clements/Sipa USA/AP Images, 27

Editor: Patrick Donnelly
Series Designer: Craig Hinton

Publisher's Cataloging-in-Publication Data

Names: Hall, Brian, author.
Title: NFL's top 10 comebacks / by Brian Hall.
Other titles: NFL's top ten comebacks
Description: Minneapolis, MN : Abdo Publishing, 2018. | Series: NFL's top 10 |
    Includes bibliographical references and index.
Identifiers: LCCN 2016963091 | ISBN 9781532111396 (lib. bdg.) |
    ISBN 9781680789249 (ebook)
Subjects: LCSH: National Football League--Juvenile literature. | Football--
    --United States--History--Juvenile literature. | Football--United States--
    Miscellanea--Juvenile literature. | Football--United States--Statistics--Juvenile
    literature. | Sports comebacks--United States--Juvenile literature.
Classification: DDC 796.332--dc23
LC record available at http://lccn.loc.gov/2016963091

Table of
CONTENTS

Introduction

Some National Football League (NFL) games are known simply by the nicknames they've been given. Fans still talk about legendary comebacks such as the "Music City Miracle" and "The Drive." Many of those games are remembered for the quarterbacks who led the winning drives. Joe Montana and John Elway were famous for bringing their teams back when all hope appeared lost.

It's difficult to narrow down a list of the NFL's greatest comebacks because there have been so many. The games in this list were chosen for their historical impact. Playoff games take on added significance. The size of the deficit and time left in the game also factor into the discussion.

Here are the top 10 comebacks in NFL history.

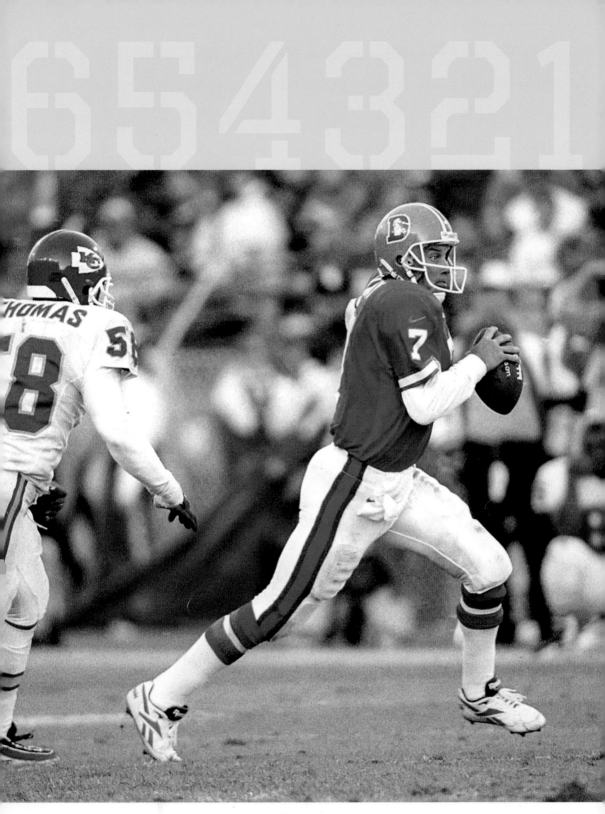

10

Jeff Garcia celebrates his touchdown run in the fourth quarter of the 49ers' victory over the New York Giants. →

Garcia Joins the Greats

Joe Montana and Steve Young are remembered as two of the greatest quarterbacks ever to play in the NFL. Montana led the San Francisco 49ers to four Super Bowl victories in the 1980s. Young replaced Montana and was named the NFL's Most Valuable Player (MVP) twice. He also was named MVP of the Super Bowl as San Francisco won its fifth title.

Jeff Garcia had the tough job of trying to replace the two Hall of Famers. Garcia didn't match the success that Montana and Young had in San Francisco. But he was a huge part of the second-biggest playoff comeback ever.

The 49ers hosted the New York Giants in the first round of the National Football Conference (NFC) playoffs after the 2002 season. New York led 38–14 with just over four minutes left in the third quarter. But Garcia wouldn't let the Niners go quietly. Terrell Owens caught his second touchdown of the game to start the comeback near the end of the third quarter. Garcia ran for a touchdown on the first play of the fourth quarter. Then, after the Niners added a field goal, Garcia connected with wide receiver Tai Streets for a 13-yard touchdown pass. With one minute left in the game, San Francisco had rallied to take a 39–38 lead.

Then things *really* got crazy. New York quarterback Kerry Collins drove the Giants down the field quickly. Kicker Matt Bryant lined up a potential game-winning field goal from 40 yards out. But holder Matt Allen couldn't handle a bad snap. Allen scrambled right and heaved a pass into the end zone as time expired. But it fell incomplete, and San Francisco celebrated an amazing comeback victory.

9

Travis Benjamin hauls in a touchdown as the Browns rally against Tennessee. →

Surprise Shootout

Classic NFL comebacks often involve star quarterbacks excelling in pressure situations. But an early-October game between two non-playoff teams became one of the most exciting games in NFL history.

The Cleveland Browns finished the 2014 season with a 7–9 record. That doesn't sound too impressive, but it was their best record in seven years. A midseason comeback on the road against the Tennessee Titans was the highlight of the Browns' season.

Journeyman quarterback Charlie Whitehurst had replaced injured Titans starter Jake Locker. Another longtime backup quarterback, Brian Hoyer, was under center for Cleveland. Neither player had shown much

The Titans had plenty to celebrate early in their 2014 game against the Browns.

8

to indicate an exciting shootout would unfold, but that's exactly what they delivered.

Whitehurst threw two touchdown passes in the second quarter as Tennessee took a 28–3 lead. Then Hoyer threw a touchdown pass to tight end Jim Dray with 16 seconds left before halftime. It was a sign of things to come. The Browns got a field goal in the third quarter to make the score 28–13. They inched closer when linebacker Tank Carder blocked a Tennessee punt out of the end zone for a safety.

Then Hoyer and wide receiver Travis Benjamin went to work. As the Cleveland defense continued to stop the Titans' offense, Hoyer threw two touchdown passes to Benjamin in the final seven minutes to give Cleveland a 29–28 win. The 25-point comeback was the biggest by a road team in NFL history.

8

The scoreboard tells the story as 49ers fans storm the field after the 1981 NFC Championship Game.

Clark Makes "The Catch"

It's not often that you can pinpoint the moment when one dynasty ends and the next one begins. But that's what happened in the NFC Championship Game following the 1981 season. The Dallas Cowboys were known as "America's Team." They had played in the Super Bowl five times over a nine-year span. But the San Francisco 49ers were a team on the rise.

San Francisco had gone 2–14 in 1978 and 1979. Then Coach Bill Walsh led a quick turnaround, guiding the Niners to a 13–3 record in 1981. Now they had to get past Dallas in the playoffs to claim the NFC title.

The lead changed hands six times in an evenly matched game. The Cowboys led 27–21 with just under five minutes to play. The 49ers had the ball at their own 11-yard line. Quarterback Joe Montana would have to lead his team 89 yards for a touchdown. And that's what he did. Over 12 plays, the Niners marched to the Dallas 6-yard line with 58 seconds left.

On the next play, Montana drifted to his right to give himself more time to find a receiver. Three Cowboys closed in on the quarterback. Finally, Montana lofted the ball high to the back of the end zone. It looked like the pass would sail out of the end zone. But then wide receiver Dwight Clark appeared to come out of nowhere, leaping high to pull in the touchdown. Ray Wersching's extra-point kick gave the 49ers a 28–27 lead.

CAPTAIN COMEBACK

Montana was known as "Joe Cool" for being a master of the comeback. In 1980 he brought San Francisco back from a 28-point deficit to beat the New Orleans Saints. It was the largest regular-season comeback in NFL history. Montana also drove the 49ers 92 yards in the final minutes to win the Super Bowl in January 1989.

The comeback was nearly complete. Dallas tried to get in position for a field goal, but the San Francisco defense forced a fumble at midfield. Defensive lineman Jim Stuckey recovered it, and the 49ers were on their way to their first Super Bowl, where they beat the Cincinnati Bengals. That marked the beginning of a new period of dominance, as the 49ers won three more Super Bowls over the next eight seasons.

7

Jumbo Elliott, *76*, and Vinny Testaverde celebrate their unlikely touchdown hookup that sent the Jets-Dolphins game into overtime in 2000.

Vinny and the Monday Night Miracle

Vinny Testaverde was the first pick of the 1987 NFL Draft. His career never lived up to that lofty status, but the quarterback's performance one Monday night in 2000 was unforgettable.

The Miami Dolphins led the New York Jets 30–7 with 12 seconds left in the third quarter. That's when Testaverde rallied the Jets in front of their home crowd. He threw touchdown passes to wide receiver Laveranues Coles and tight end Jermaine Wiggins. John Hall kicked a field goal. And Miami couldn't make a first down on offense.

When Testaverde hit wide receiver Wayne Chrebet for a 24-yard touchdown, the Jets had tied the game 30–30. But almost four minutes remained, and on Miami's next play, quarterback Jay Fiedler threw a 46-yard touchdown pass. The Jets got the ball back with 3:22 to play. Testaverde had to orchestrate another rally.

A long kickoff return gave New York the ball at its 43-yard line. Testaverde completed six of seven passes on the drive. He then connected with John "Jumbo" Elliott for a 3-yard touchdown to tie the game again. Elliott was an offensive tackle who had reported as an eligible receiver. It was the only catch Elliott would make during his 14-year NFL career.

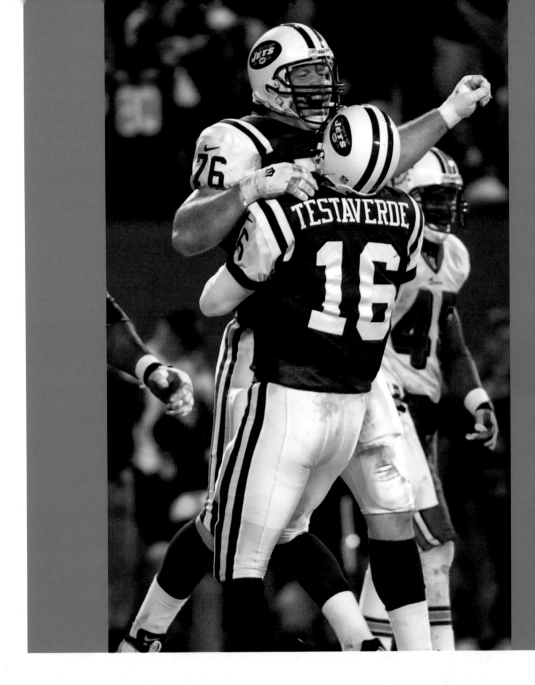

Miami got the ball first in overtime, but the Jets intercepted a Fiedler pass. Three Testaverde completions led to Hall's 40-yard game-winning field goal. Testaverde finished with 378 passing yards and threw five touchdown passes, the only five-touchdown game of his 21-year career.

6

Devin Hester, *23*, outruns the Arizona defenders on his game-winning punt return in 2006. →

Cards Let Bears Escape

NFL coaches have issued plenty of famous postgame rants throughout the years. Few match the outburst from Arizona Cardinals coach Dennis Green after his team lost to the Chicago Bears in 2006.

The Bears came into the Monday night game 5–0, but their winning streak appeared to be in grave danger in the Arizona desert. The Cardinals led 23–3 late in the third quarter, and their defense was giving the Bears fits. Chicago turned the ball over six times, with quarterback Rex Grossman throwing four interceptions.

But instead of rolling over, the Bears' defense took over. On the last snap of the third quarter, defensive end Mark Anderson sacked Cardinals quarterback Matt Leinart and caused a fumble. Chicago safety Mike Brown recovered the ball and returned it for a touchdown.

Cardinals coach Dennis Green wasn't impressed with what he saw from his team against the Bears.

With 5:11 left in the game, Arizona running back Edgerrin James fumbled. Bears cornerback Charles Tillman scooped up the ball and ran 40 yards for another touchdown. The comeback was completed when the Bears forced an Arizona punt that Devin Hester returned 83 yards for a touchdown. The Cardinals missed a field goal with less than a minute to play, sealing Chicago's improbable 24–23 victory.

Green's irritability in the postgame press conference was understandable. His team had surrendered a big lead in an unlikely fashion. The Bears won despite gaining just 168 yards on offense. Green and his coaches had put together a winning game plan, only to see it fall apart in the end. He couldn't contain his anger when he addressed the media after the game.

"They are who we thought they were! And we let 'em off the hook!" Green yelled before leaving the podium.

Arizona ended up finishing the season 5–11, and Green was fired. The Bears went 13–3 and lost to the Indianapolis Colts in the Super Bowl.

5

John Elway fires a pass against the Browns in overtime of the 1986 AFC Championship Game.

Elway Drives Broncos

Denver Broncos quarterback John Elway was legendary for his comeback victories. He will forever be a villain in Cleveland after the way he took down the Browns.

The Browns went 13–3 in 1986 and were primed to reach their first Super Bowl. They hosted the Broncos in the American Football Conference (AFC) Championship Game. Quarterback Bernie Kosar threw a 48-yard touchdown pass to wide receiver Brian Brennan in the fourth quarter, giving Cleveland a 20–13 lead. The Broncos got the ball at their own 2-yard line with 5:32 left in the game. Just enough time for "The Drive."

Elway led Denver's offense onto the field. On a frigid January day, the 26-year-old quarterback marched the Broncos 98 yards in 15 plays. Elway was 6-for-9 passing on the drive, and he ran twice for 20 yards. He kept the drive alive with a 20-yard pass to Mark Jackson on third-and-18. Five plays later, Jackson caught a 5-yard touchdown pass with 31 seconds remaining.

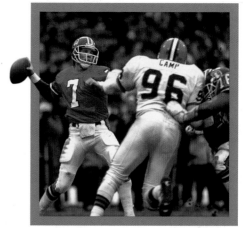

"THE FUMBLE"

A year later, the Browns looked ready to return the favor in Denver in the AFC Championship Game. Trailing 38–31 with just over a minute to play, Cleveland had the ball at Denver's 8-yard line. Running back Earnest Byner took a handoff and surged toward the goal line. But cornerback Jeremiah Castille stripped the ball, and the Broncos recovered. The play became known as "The Fumble," and it prevented the Browns from turning the tables one year after "The Drive."

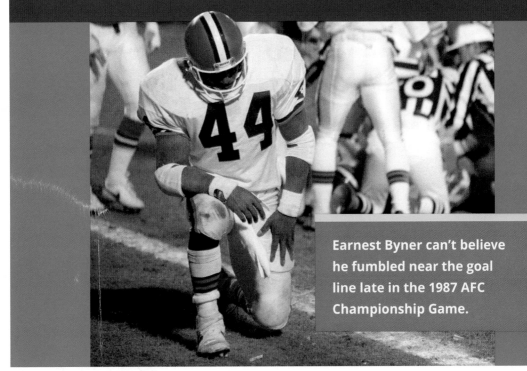

Earnest Byner can't believe he fumbled near the goal line late in the 1987 AFC Championship Game.

Rich Karlis tied the game with the point-after kick. Elway then took Denver 60 yards in nine plays in overtime to set up Karlis's 33-yard, game-winning field goal. The Broncos lost to the New York Giants in the Super Bowl, but Elway had established himself as a quarterback no defense wanted to face with the game on the line.

4

Tennessee's Kevin Dyson runs down the sideline, shocking the Bills with the "Music City Miracle" in the 1999 AFC playoffs. →

"Miracle" Play Saves Titans

Nashville, Tennessee, is home to the NFL's Titans. It's also known as "Music City" for its connection to the music industry. A 1999 AFC playoff game between the Titans and Buffalo Bills produced a play that NFL fans have been talking about ever since.

The Titans trailed Buffalo by a point with 16 seconds to play. They didn't need a long drive—they needed a miracle. Bills kicker Steve Christie had just given Buffalo a 16–15 lead with a 41-yard field goal. Christie sent the ensuing kickoff high and short. Fullback Lorenzo Neal fielded the kick at the Titans 25-yard line and handed off to tight end Frank Wycheck. Wycheck ran to his right, pulling the Bills defenders with him. Then he turned and threw the ball across the field to receiver Kevin Dyson. Dyson caught the ball at his feet and came up running.

The field opened up for Dyson as he sprinted down the left sideline. The Bills were completely fooled. Dyson picked up blockers on his way to the end zone for a touchdown. There were no flags on the play. After a long review, the officials ruled the play was legal, and the Titans ended up winning 22–16.

The "Music City Miracle" remains one of the most controversial plays in NFL history. Wycheck's pass across the field was close to going forward. A lateral is illegal if it goes forward. Wycheck threw the ball from just past the 25-yard line. Dyson caught it just past the 25-yard line, so the call stood.

Andrew Luck throws a pass against Kansas City during the Colts' big playoff comeback. →

Colts Try Their Luck

The Indianapolis Colts selected one of the best quarterback prospects in years with the top pick in the 2012 NFL Draft. It didn't take Andrew Luck long to prove himself, especially in close games. He led 11 game-winning drives in the fourth quarter in his first two seasons.

Luck's best comeback of all came in the playoffs after his second season. Luck and the Colts were facing a 28-point deficit at home against the Kansas City Chiefs. Kansas City quarterback Alex Smith's fourth touchdown pass gave the Chiefs a 38–10 lead early in the third quarter.

Running back Donald Brown teamed with Luck to bring the Colts back. Brown scored consecutive touchdowns in the third quarter. Brown's second touchdown was a pass from Luck. Soon after, Luck connected with tight end Coby Fleener for another touchdown and then alertly picked up a fumble and scored a rushing touchdown. The Colts trailed 41–38 with more than 10 minutes to play.

The Chiefs added a field goal on their next drive, but Indianapolis responded quickly. Luck completed the comeback with a 64-yard touchdown pass to T. Y. Hilton with 4:21 left for a 45–44 lead. The Chiefs drove into Colts territory, but the Indianapolis defense held, and the Colts came away with an unlikely victory.

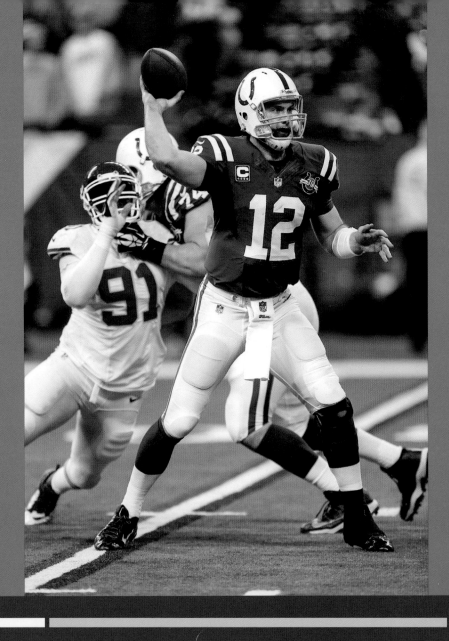

IN GOOD HANDS

Indianapolis drafted quarterback Peyton Manning with the first pick in the draft in 1998. Manning was named first-team All-Pro seven times and led the team to two Super Bowls, winning one in February 2007. A neck injury sidelined Manning for the entire 2011 season. The Colts went 2–14, got the top pick in the draft, and used it to acquire Luck.

2

Andre Reed, *right*, scores one of his three touchdowns. →

Buffalo Blitz

In January 1993, the Buffalo Bills were looking to win their third straight AFC title. The road to the Super Bowl began with a wild-card playoff game at home against the Houston Oilers.

But the Bills were almost derailed before they started. Oilers quarterback Warren Moon threw four touchdown passes as Houston went into halftime with a 28–3 lead. The outlook got worse for Buffalo after Oilers safety Bubba McDowell returned an interception for a touchdown early in the second half for a 35–3 lead. Along the way, Buffalo had also lost star running back Thurman Thomas to injury. The Bills were already playing without Hall of Fame quarterback Jim Kelly, who had been injured the week before. When Thomas went down, all hope appeared lost.

But then backup quarterback Frank Reich caught fire. He threw three touchdown passes in the third quarter, two of them to Andre Reed, to cut Houston's lead to 35–31. Houston drove into field-goal range early in the fourth quarter. But the holder bobbled the snap on the field-goal attempt, and the Oilers didn't score. The Bills pounced on the mistake. Reed scored his third straight touchdown on a 17-yard pass from Reich, and Buffalo led 38–35.

Now Moon had a chance at leading his own comeback. The Oilers reached the Buffalo 9-yard line, but they had to settle for an Al Del Greco 26-yard field goal to tie the game and force overtime. The Oilers got the ball first, but on their third play from scrimmage, Bills cornerback Nate Odomes intercepted a Moon pass deep in Oilers territory. Steve Christie kicked a 32-yard field goal for the win. The 32-point comeback was the biggest in NFL history in either the regular season or the playoffs.

1

Matt Ryan, *left*, and Tevin Coleman had the Falcons rolling early.

Brady Bounces Back

uper Bowl LI in February 2017 was a classic matchup. Quarterback Matt Ryan led the high-flying Atlanta Falcons. He had won the NFL's MVP Award after throwing for 38 touchdowns and nearly 5,000 yards. The New England Patriots, meanwhile, had the NFL's best defense and a top-10 rushing attack. The Patriots also had four-time Super Bowl champion quarterback Tom Brady.

Brady was 39 years old. But as Atlanta would soon find out, you can never bet against Brady.

Neither team could get much going in the first quarter, but then the Falcons began to click on offense. Devonta Freeman scored the game's first touchdown on a 5-yard run early in the second quarter. Then Ryan threw a 19-yard scoring strike to Austin Hooper that gave the Falcons a 14–0 lead.

Tom Brady's diving effort comes up short as Robert Alford sprints toward the end zone with a second-quarter interception.

Suddenly the pressure was on the Patriots. No team had ever come back from more than 10 points down to win the Super Bowl. Even worse, Brady was starting to look rattled. The Falcons defense was putting constant pressure on him. Soon, disaster struck. Brady's short pass to his left was off target. Cornerback Robert Alford intercepted it at the Atlanta 18-yard line and started running the other way. Alford rolled to the end zone untouched. His 82-yard return gave Atlanta a 21–0 lead.

The Patriots managed to drive for a field goal before halftime, but the Falcons' 21–3 lead appeared safe. And it looked even better when Ryan found Tevin Coleman for a 6-yard touchdown pass. Atlanta led 28–3 with 8:31 left in the third quarter.

Surely the Patriots were dead in the water, right?

Wrong. Brady suddenly looked like a different player. He marched the Patriots 75 yards, capping the drive with a 5-yard touchdown pass to

James White. Then, after a defensive stop, New England added another field goal.

The Patriots were trailing 28–12 early in the fourth quarter when they got their big break. Linebacker Dont'a Hightower flew around the left end and blasted Ryan. The ball popped out and defensive tackle Alan Branch recovered it at the Atlanta 25-yard line. Five plays later, Brady connected with Danny Amendola on a 6-yard touchdown pass. White ran up the middle for the two-point conversion. Suddenly it was 28–20 with 5:56 to play. The Patriots were within one score, and the Falcons were reeling.

But Ryan settled their nerves. He completed two long passes to move the Falcons into field-goal range. With Pro Bowl kicker Matt Bryant on their side, odds were good that Atlanta would soon extend its lead to at least 11 points and crush the Patriots' comeback.

However, Ryan was sacked for a loss of 12 yards. Then a holding penalty pushed the Falcons even farther back. They had to punt. Brady got the ball back with 3:30 to play at his own 9-yard line. The Patriots had to go 91 yards for a touchdown and get another two-point conversion to tie the game.

And that's just what they did. Brady picked apart the exhausted Atlanta defense. Wide receiver Julian Edelman made a diving catch of a deflected pass to give New England the ball at the Atlanta 41. Brady completed three straight passes before White surged for a 1-yard touchdown run. When Amendola caught a bullet from Brady and dipped across the goal line, the game was tied 28–28.

The Patriots had come back from 25 points down. But they weren't done. New England won the overtime coin toss and elected to receive. The weary Falcons defenders were no match for the energized Brady, who completed five straight passes to get the ball to the Atlanta 25. White then ran for 10 yards. A pass interference penalty put the Patriots at the 2-yard line. And two plays later, White fought through a tackle and dived into the end zone for the final score.

After falling behind 28–3, Brady had gone 26-for-33 for 284 yards. He threw for Super Bowl–record 466 yards and was named the game's MVP. He also earned his fifth Super Bowl ring, more than any other quarterback, and proved why it's never smart to bet against him.

James White, 28, splits the Falcons defense for the game-winning touchdown.

Honorable Mentions

GIANTS 17, PATRIOTS 14: There haven't been many big comebacks in the Super Bowl. There has been plenty of late-game drama, though. Eli Manning and the New York Giants provided some in 2008 when they ended the New England Patriots' chance at an undefeated season. Manning led New York to the game-winning touchdown on a drive most known for receiver David Tyree's amazing catch. Tyree pinned the ball against his helmet as he was being brought down by defenders to set up Manning's game-winning touchdown pass to Plaxico Burress.

49ERS 20, BENGALS 16: Winning the Super Bowl in January 1989 might have been Joe Montana's career masterpiece. Cincinnati led by three points with 3:20 left in the game. The 49ers needed to drive 92 yards for the win. Montana completed eight of nine passes and finished the drive with a 10-yard touchdown pass to John Taylor with just 34 seconds left.

STEELERS 27, CARDINALS 23: Arizona was looking for its first Super Bowl win in 2009. But Pittsburgh quarterback Ben Roethlisberger led a 78-yard drive in the final two minutes. He connected with Santonio Holmes in the back corner of the end zone for the game-winning 6-yard touchdown pass.

BILLS 37, COLTS 35: Most big comebacks are done with quarterbacks leading big passing games. Buffalo took a different route in a 1997 regular-season game. Running back Antowain Smith led the Bills back from a 26–0 deficit. Buffalo started the turnaround in the second quarter. Smith scored three second-half touchdowns to go with 129 rushing yards.

BRONCOS 35, CHARGERS 24: Peyton Manning's biggest comeback was in an October 2012 game at San Diego. Manning's Broncos were losing 24–0 at halftime on the road. Manning threw three touchdown passes, and the Broncos forced five turnovers in the second half. Denver scored twice on defense in what turned out to be a decisive 35–24 victory.

PATRIOTS 34, BRONCOS 31: A year later, Manning and the Broncos were on the opposite side against another star quarterback. Denver stormed to a 24–0 halftime lead in New England. But Tom Brady threw three touchdown passes in the second half as the Patriots scored 31 straight points. Manning threw a touchdown pass to send the game into overtime. But Denver fumbled a punt deep in its own territory late in overtime. New England got a field goal from Stephen Gostkowski to win 34–31.

LIONS 31, 49ERS 27: San Francisco hosted Detroit in a 1957 playoff game to determine the champion of the NFL's Western Division. The 49ers surged to a 24–7 halftime lead thanks to three touchdown passes by quarterback Y. A. Tittle. They extended their cushion to 27–7 in the third quarter before the Lions came roaring back. Running back Tom Tracy scored two touchdowns and teammate Gene Gedman added another as Detroit rallied for a 31–27 win. The next week the Lions beat the Cleveland Browns to win the NFL title.

Glossary

comeback
When a team losing a game rallies to take the lead.

controversy
Unwanted disagreement or negative attention.

decade
A span of 10 years.

deficit
The amount by which a team is trailing in a game.

dynasty
A team that has an extended period of success, usually winning multiple championships in the process.

journeyman
A player who has played for many teams or has been unable to find a specific role.

lateral
A pass that goes sideways or backward.

momentum
The sense that a team is playing well and will be difficult to stop.

rant
To talk loudly, usually to stress or focus on a particular point.

torment
Cause trouble, pain, or sadness.

turnover
Loss of the ball to the other team through an interception or fumble.

For More Information

Books

Bryant, Howard. *Legends: The Best Players, Games, and Teams in Football*. New York: Philomel Books, 2015.

Kelley, K. C. *Football Superstars 2016*. New York: Scholastic Inc., 2016.

The Editors of Sports Illustrated Kids. *Sports Illustrated Kids 1st and 10: Top 10 Lists of Everything in Football*. New York: Time Home Entertainment, 2016.

Websites

To learn more about the NFL, visit **abdobooklinks.com**. These links are routinely monitored and updated to provide the most current information available.

Place to Visit

Pro Football Hall of Fame
2121 George Halas Drive NW
Canton, Ohio 44708
330-456-8207
www.profootballhof.com

Built in 1963, the Pro Football Hall of Fame celebrates the best football players ever to play the game. Up to seven inductees are enshrined each year. The purpose of the hall is to honor the heroes of the game, preserve its history, promote its values, and celebrate its excellence.

Index

About the Author

Brian Hall is a sports reporter who graduated from the University of Minnesota following a stint in the United States Army. He lives in Minnesota with his wife and two kids.